# WORLD CUP WOMEN
## Megan, Alex, and the Team USA Soccer Champs

Meg Walters
Illustrated By
Nikkolas Smith

Sky Pony Press
New York

# The Team.   The Dream.
## The World Cup Heroes.

This is the story of twenty-three girls who worked together to become the heroes of USA soccer.

They came from all over the country. Some had purple hair, some had curly hair. Some were tall, and some short . . .

. . . but despite their differences, they were excited to join forces to get to the top, to take first place, to leave their marks on the world.

**Each player can remember the exact moment she declared...**

"I want to be a professional soccer player when I grow up!"

Megan Rapinoe grew up in Redding, California, with five brothers and sisters. She and her twin sister, Rachael, would play soccer together in their backyard, and their dad coached their soccer teams.

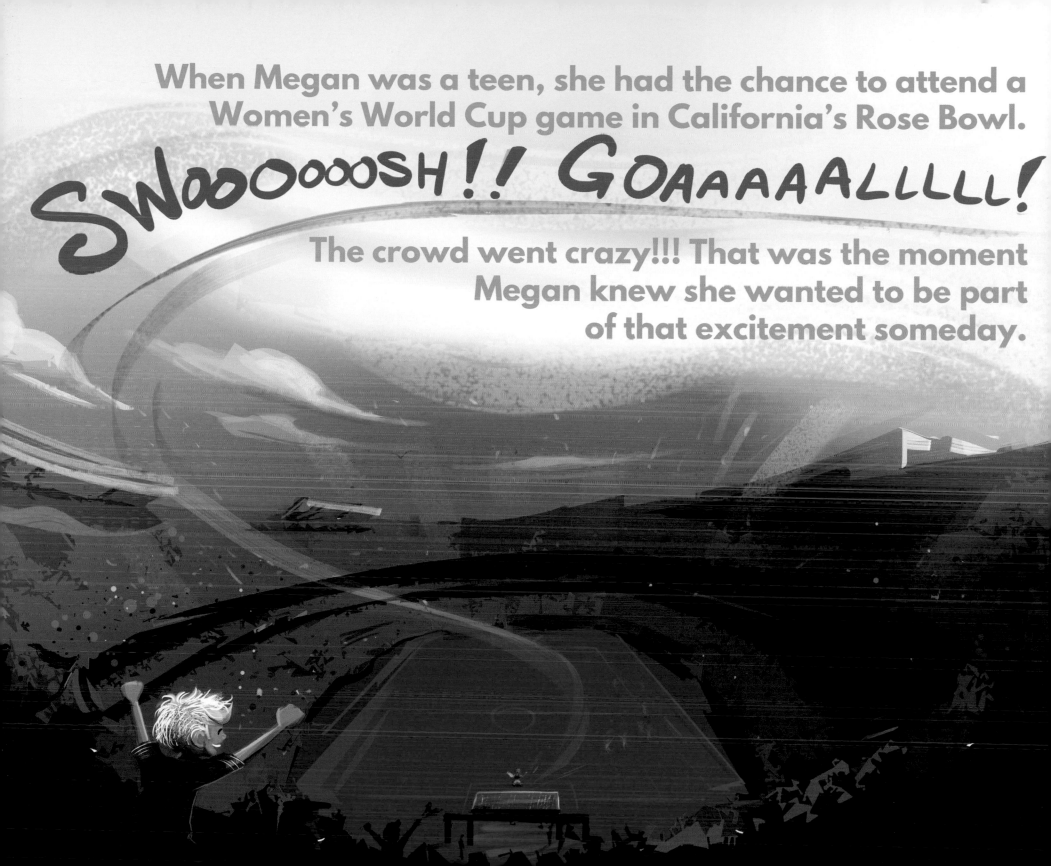

In Diamond Bar, California, a little girl named Alex Morgan dreamed of becoming a soccer player, too.
Alex loved to play all types of sports with her older sisters.

When she was very young, she watched the US Women's Team win the 1999 World Cup on TV. The strength, the skill, the teamwork that went into that win—Alex wanted that, too.

Julie, Tobin, Crystal, Abby...
they all practiced year-round, for long hours.

Kelley, Becky, Lindsey, Alyssa, and Rose...
they were all dedicated to becoming the best
soccer players they could be.

# Finally, their big day arrived.

FRANCE　　ITALY　　NORWAY　　JAPAN　　SOUTH AFRICA　　SPAIN

AUSTRALIA　　USA　　CAMEROON　　SCOTLAND　　CHILE　　CANADA

The World Cup Championship was held in
Paris, France, in the summer of 2019.

BRAZIL   NIGERIA   GERMANY   CHINA   NEW ZEALAND   SWEDEN

ENGLAND   ARGENTINA   SOUTH KOREA   JAMAICA   NETHERLANDS   THAILAND

Twenty-four teams from around the
world came to play.

First, team USA defeated Thailand, 13–0 . . .

then Chile, 3–0.

ROLL

Next, they beat Sweden, 2–0 . . .

DRIBBLE

then Spain, 2-1.

Then they prevailed over France, 2–1 . . .

next, England, 2–1.

. . . And on July 7, 2019, they played the Netherlands in the final game. Megan Rapinoe and Rose Lavelle each scored a goal for a 2–0 win!!

Team USA WON the World Cup, becoming the first team in history to win four Women's World Cup titles!

The team flew home to the United States, where a parade was held in their honor. They floated down the Canyon of Heroes in New York City! Thousands of soccer fans showered the team with confetti, and the mayor gave the players keys to the city.

They celebrated, they danced, and Megan even gave a speech: "This is my charge to everyone. We have to be better. We have to LOVE more. Hate less.... Yes, we play sports. Yes, we play soccer. Yes, we're female athletes. But we're so much more than that. You're so much more than that."

This team of twenty-three women was on top of the world! They won the FIFA World Cup in the biggest match of their careers, and they brought their country together, too.

United, their fellow citizens cheered them on with pride. The team lifted America's soccer program to new heights, made a case for equal pay rights, and became a shining example of what amazing things women can do individually and when they work together.

= PAY!

# WE ARE ONE NATION. WE ARE ONE TEAM.

**1**
Alyssa Naeher
Stratford, CT

**18**
Ashlyn Harris
Cocoa Beach, FL

**21**
Adrianna Franch
Salina, KS

**5**
Kelley O'Hara
Fayetteville, GA

**14**
Emily Sonnett
Marietta, GA

**7**
Abby Dahlkemper
Menlo Park, CA

**11**
Ali Krieger
Alexandria, VA

**12**
Tierna Davidson
Menlo Park, CA

**4**
Becky Sauerbrunn
(co-captain)
St. Louis, MO

**19**
Crystal Dunn
Rockville Centre,
NY

**3**
Sam Mewis
Hanson, MA

**6**
Morgan Brian
St. Simon's Island,
GA

# WE ARE THE HEROES OF AMERICAN SOCCER!

**8**
Julie Ertz
Mesa, AZ

**9**
Lindsey Horan
Golden, CO

**16**
Rose Lavelle
Cincinnati, OH

**20**
Allie Long
Huntington, NY

**2**
Mallory Pugh
Highlands Ranch, CO

**10**
Carli Lloyd
(co-captain)
Delran Township, NJ

**13**
Alex Morgan
(co-captain)
Diamond Bar, CA

**15**
Megan Rapinoe
(co-captain)
Redding, CA

**17**
Tobin Heath
Basking Ridge, NJ

**22**
Jessica McDonald
Phoenix, AZ

**23**
Christen Press
Palos Verdes, CA

Head Coach, Jill Ellis
Cowplain, England, UK
Now lives in
Palmetto Bay, FL

Dedicated to Eliza,
and to all the girls who believe they CAN.
—M.W.

For every fearless girl in the world,
turning her big dreams into reality.
—N.S.

Sky Pony Press books may be purchased in bulk at special discounts for sales promotion, corporate gifts, fund-raising, or educational purposes. Special editions can also be created to specifications. For details, contact the Special Sales Department, Sky Pony Press, 307 West 36th Street, 11th Floor, New York, NY 10018 or info@skyhorsepublishing.com.

Sky Pony® is a registered trademark of Skyhorse Publishing, Inc.®, a Delaware corporation.

Visit our website at www.skyponypress.com.

10 9 8 7 6 5

Library of Congress Cataloging-in-Publication Data is available on file.

Cover design by Nikkolas Smith/Daniel Brount
Cover illustration by Nikkolas Smith

Print ISBN: 978-1-5107-5629-8
eBook ISBN: 978-1-5107-5630-4

Printed in China